THROUGH ALL THE SPACES

THROUGH ALL THE SEASONS

THROUGH ALL THE SPACES

by

Alison Chisholm

First published in 2024
by Caleta Publishing

Copyright © Alison Chisholm 2024

The moral right of the author has been asserted.

This book is sold subject to the condition that no part of it shall be reproduced, stored in a retrieval system (other than for the purposes of review), or transmitted in any form or by any means, electronic, mechanical, photocopying, recording or otherwise, without the prior permission in writing of the copyright owner.

ISBN   978-1-4452-5502-6

Cover photograph by Alison Chisholm

Printed and bound by Lulu.com

ACKNOWLEDGEMENTS

Some of these poems have appeared in Reach, Common Threads, Orbis, Different Days, and The Poet's A-Z, have won awards in the National Federation of State Poetry Societies and Ohio Poetry Day competitions, or have been broadcast by BBC Radio Merseyside.

OTHER COLLECTIONS
BY ALISON CHISHOLM

Alone No More (with Robin Gregory)
Flying Free
The Need for Unicorns
Single Return
Light Angles
Daring the Slipstream
Mapping the Maze
Hold Tight
Iced
Star and Snowflake
A Fraction from Parallel
Echoes in Cloud
Mistletoe and Manger

For Emma and Jeff, Julia and Ian

4th MAY 1970

A waning crescent moon drips pallid light,
enough to make the diamond sparkle on my finger,
each facet angling to stir colour
from dusk's greying. You
take my hand, turn it, kiss the palm,
make this ordinary street a place
of milk and honey promises.

We talk in unlearned tones,
abstract hopes for dreams we can't imagine
on a surreal evening in an unreal life.

Tomorrow will bring its awakening
to brick and mortar facts, truths
about work, insurance, shopping for food, trappings
to tie us down. But tonight
will stay at the centre, fix us,
echo its love to resound through all the spaces.

HAIKU

Twilight: the river
holds its breath, anticipates
a ripple of swan.

SUMMONED BY WOLVES

There are no wolves here, so why
did distant howling disturb my dreams?
What made me pull on jeans and sweater,
leave my home's warmth,
walk into the wood where moonlight silvered trees?

I sensed new urgency in the calling, wondered
if a pack of dogs was loose; knew
it must be something worse, knew that I was being drawn
toward the sound. Twigs cracked beneath my feet;
an owl, silent-winged, glided past my face. I felt
no fear, but only a need to hurry through the pines,
their rain-stung resin filling my head.

I was getting nearer, aware
of bats criss-crossing moonbeams,
and at once I was afraid, so scared
I trembled, stumbled, steadied myself
against a fir's rough trunk.

That's when I saw them, wolf shapes
filling shadows, throwing back their heads
to howl, teeth gleaming.

They saw me too, stopped as one beast,
turned to look, thirty eyes pricking the woodlight,
fifteen mouths slavering, fifteen pelts bristling.

As the first leapt
I felt hot sourness of its breath,
the weight of great paws at my shoulders,
thud of the earth's shudder when I fell.

It was morning when I realised
I was still alive, still breathing,
scenting new freshness in the forest air,
sensing a strange oneness with the pack.

I stood up slowly, gingerly, amazed
a dull ache was the only sign
of last night's horror. Now
I felt connected, felt that I belonged.

Retracing the route, I found myself back home,
surprised myself by making toast and coffee,
showering, changing; surprised myself by realising
I yearned for night to come again,
by longing for the next full moon.

HOLY GROUND

They built a shop where the church once stood,
centre of town, bulldozing brick and stone,
smashing glass that used to bring light
to touch the eyes of worshippers. They ploughed
pew and altar into ballast, wrenched
walls bereft of reverence, pulped bibles
and hymnbooks, collapsed symbols of the faith
that could move mountains.

Concrete and faceless, the shop boasted rank
upon rank of dresses, shirts and trousers,
Disney-motif pyjamas; cut price candles
and cushions and throws filled shelves.
It was only at night as the last staff
were leaving, laboured breathing wheezed
down aisles smug with socks and gloves,
behind counters where the faithful
made their oblations. Only then
did a rustling stir, making dresses ripple,
tipping hangers, shaking garish garments
to the floor.

The early shift muttered
about localised earth tremors,
grumbled as they collected up
swathes of stock, replaced it on hangers.
The third time builders were blamed.
Were the floors uneven?
It took a month for someone to mention
Poltergeist, another for exorcism
to be voiced.

They tried for decades – new suggestions,
new solutions. The shop, in prime position
on the main road, changed hands;
and again; and again.

Sixty years on, the concrete facade
looks tired. The whole road is in decline
as online purchases dig the graves
for the High Street stores. And now
as they turn out the lights and lock the doors,
before the nightly descent of stock,
there is a sound not of laboured breathing,
but the joyous swell of triumphant hymns.

FAIRYTALE

I've read the stories, know the rituals. She'll think
this is a gentle stroll, a walk through springy meadows
listening to birdsong, counting blossoms.
We'll reach the wood before she realises.

Strange she's picked today to reminisce. Her memories
of lazy summer picnics are not mine. I recall
the wasps, spilt lemonade, dried and curling sandwiches.
I'll say nothing – let her have this hour.

We're nearly at the first straggling pines,
can see the path that darkens where it narrows.
I'll slow my pace a fraction, let her get ahead.
It's worked. She's five steps further off, prattling
about squirrels. Fitting, that this final walk is stilted with trivia.

That's how I knew there was no way forward,
when every conversation revolved around her,
her meals, her worries, how it took such time to choose
her clothes each day; as if it mattered.
When her sentences descended into querulous rambling,
when she forgot how to break an egg or sign a cheque,
I knew there was nothing left for her.

She'll find a bar of chocolate in her bag, a small bottle
of water. I'm not cruel. She's wandered further.
I can only just make out her yellow jacket through the trees.
I step back slowly, eyes fixed on her diminishing form,
don't turn until she's out of sight.

I check the way we came, make sure
she's dropped no breadcrumbs,
unravelled no cardigan
of threads to guide her back.

Bright day beckons. April lightens the air,
lightens my step. I skim across the meadow,
making plans. I'll wait a day or two, ring the police,
feign concern, tell how she left to visit friends,
never arrived. And I'll be free.

BLANK PAGE

I glare at it. It glares back,
commanding more menace
than a sheet of paper should.
I know my enemy, but it knows me better.
It has squared up to battle
several million times
before it had to face me.

It remembers Ts'ai Lun
mixing mulberry bark and hemp,
rags and water, pulping, pressing
and hanging it to dry,
then searching for something to write about.

It remembers papyrus,
woven strands of pithy sedge
formed, pressed, dried
in order to challenge scribes
to find the words to fill it.

It remembers vellum,
calf skins cleaned, bleached, stretched,
scraped, scratched with pumice,
treated with lime; and its coarser fellow,
parchment, anticipating magic words
that would make it dance.

It recalls sparring
with Dante, Shakespeare, Cervantes,
with Rimbaud, Tagore, assorted Brontës,
and daring to impose
its mind-numbing blankness
to stop their Muse.

I am small fry, with my dearth of ideas,
stunted imagination. It lets me doodle
a flower in its corner, my name, the date:
knows I am not a serious contender.

CEMETERY

Beneath the great cathedral's soaring tower
a sandstone quarry gapes, that has become
a city's graveyard. Here a guide explains
how many of its bodies were the drowned
from storms that wrecked a score of ships. We learn
about the baby dragged from Mother's arms,
swept overboard. And there are orphans here,
where charity was not enough to bring
good food and healing to the children. Men
are ranked and equal, subject to death's stroke
in mausoleum or in unmarked grave.
Some lives are scarred by tragedy. A child
died aged four months, her brother at three years,
and each inscription's poignant record tells
the leveller did not discriminate.
When cholera was rife, the hearse's gate
was seldom closed, and body after body
completed final journeys at this site.
The graveyard has its heroes. One campaigned
for better sanitation for the poor,
taught cleanliness and hygiene. One became
an MP, caring of constituents,
and labouring for other people's rights.
Another turned the craft of nursing care
into a real profession. Everyone
who rests here left a mark and changed the world,
a little or a lot, by living in it.

The city's one remaining spring flows through,
a pool of life, to nourish and refresh
new generations after centuries
of nurturing vast shoals of citizens.
And now they come here walking dogs, to eat
a lunch in quiet and peace snatched from the noise
and bustle of the streets. No new graves yawn.
The cemetery is full. It soothes, it rests,
slips into history; becomes the past.

GORDIAN

Imagine this: each trouble that you bear,
each pain or problem is a Gordian knot.
Its ravelling, the root of your despair,
might take a moment or a year. Your lot
in life is governed by the way you choose
to cut or to unravel. There is speed
in slicing it in two; one slash, you lose
your burden, shed its weight, and with the deed
gain instant peace of mind. Or you could pick
at this tie, that, to ease, unloose; retain
integrity of every thread. You trick
and tease each fibre straight and smooth again.
Choose wisely. Cut – and know you've slammed the door.
Unravel – and risk knotting up once more.

MOON IN A BOTTLE

You cannot help feeling
the moon is watching you,
staring out from its bottle,
two white unblinking eyes
focussed on yours.

It dares you to interpret
the chaos in its foreground,
the unicorn, wolf, lion
camouflaged in almost-grass,
glimpses of eye and tusk,
spheres and part-spheres
two dimensions cannot flatten.

Turn to walk away,
and in turning catch
a butterfly's wing,
porcupine's crest, glow-worm.

You are drawn back
by the sheer number of green,
spot a woman, a tortoise's head,
another, bluer, unbottled moon.

Distortion of glass fascinates.
You stare at impossible stripes,
scarlet, orange, ochre, indigo,
and wonder if this is how it feels
to be hypnotised.

FLOOD

We've come a hundred miles, half way home,
when we drive into the sea. I part wake
from warm motion's nearly sleep to find
the English/Welsh border awash.

Earth-churned ripples make brown waves
encroaching on the road then trickling back,
leaving a silt of slip to be picked up
by the next surge, next car.

Nobody stops or slows. Doing so
would dice with flooding brakes, a risk
of the car not starting; and who
would paddle through mud to tut at the engine?

Bemused crows circle, deprived of roadkill,
unable to field-forage; caw their disapproval.
A pair of mallards quack contentedly.
I wonder how many mice and rabbits drown.

The road rises. I lean back to drowse again,
satisfied that recent storms burst banks here,
left more northerly rivers to their normal course.
But as my eyelids close, all I can see

is devastated families, swilling, rinsing,
disinfecting their houses, trying to salvage
undamaged possessions, knowing foundations
will never be the same again.

SEA CHANGE

They draw me in, that shimmering shoal,
writhe in wavelets around my legs,
while salt burns my throat. Their swirl
creates a vortex, prompts me
to slip beneath the surface,
open my eyes, open my mouth.

I cannot tell how long I lie there
before I realise I am breathing,
before I feel fear of sun, dry air.

I cannot remember when I shed my swim clothes,
when my hair grew, drifted, fanned.
But now I can feel my feet fuse and splay,
feel scales start from skin. I give
one tentative kick – am propelled
with ease, with speed across the bay.

Fish swim beside, around me,
and I can hear their messages,
feel their thoughts.

I reach a crop of rocks; lift my head
above water to try dryness. It breathes
as I remember from before,
but when and how are receding,
memory diminishing.

Arms I used to use to carry or embrace
assist my leap from ocean into air.
I sit, look back to the land
of an age ago, pity creatures
who have to live and die there; run fingers
through hair the colour of conch.

SEEING SATURN

Ten a penny, those pinpricks of light,
those stars, planets, sun-caught space junk,
meteors and comets – but Saturn,
now there's the real deal. I saw him once,
a twinkle in the vast black eye
of January night; would have missed him in a blink
but someone had a telescope, urged me to look.

Jolly in yellow, a bubble of helium, hydrogen,
able to float in a bathtub of water,
should a forty-thousand-mile-square tub exist,
he hula-hooped a fraction
of his thirty-year journey round the sun
as I shivered on my small blue sphere,
willing him to close the gap.

For I had seen his separate rings,
felt the spin of icy particles, some specks,
some mountains, that belied his namesake's
Golden Age, turn-of-season festival,
pledging new growth to sacrifice
to his waiting scythe. I had felt
the pull of his larger than life magnetism,
storybook image of how a planet should be.

His sweeping winds swept out my mind,
spurting moon sprayed my night.
Frozen to earth but sated, I closed my eyes
to the rest of the cosmos, knew I'd met its colossus.

NATURE STUDY

I knew the theory, abridged
when Miss Sutcliffe described
that blobs of frogspawn simply arrived,
all we needed to learn at nine. The spawn
was a mass of black dots in jelly,
waiting to grow and wiggle,
swim from the goo as tadpoles,
bud legs, lose their tails, metamorphose.

But I was greedy to see, wanted it to happen
before my eyes. I pedalled fast, a large glass jar
occupying the basket strapped to my handlebars,
bumped along the path until I spotted a pool
jewelled with spawn, wriggling
with the newly hatched. The jar was lowered,
filled, capped with a pierced lid …
and I cycled home slowly, eyes fixed
on swirling greyish liquid holding fifty new friends.

Mum found a pyrex mixing bowl,
helped me pour my precious cargo
never spilling a drop,
never dropping a tadpole. I watched
all afternoon, impatient for the limbs to grow,
longing to see real frogs; only left my post
to put my toys away before tea.

That's when it happened,
when my toddler sister, curious
from being shoo'd away, brought the jug
of her plastic tea set, plunged it in the bowl,
tested and tasted the contents.

I don't know how many she drank
before Mum, alerted by unaccustomed quiet,
spotted her and yelled. After tea
I couldn't see the bowl, guessed, as you do,
that fairies had spirited it away.

Next door's fish pond
had a lot of frogs that year.

DEPARTURE

He left slowly – began
by leaving his hat or stick behind,
losing his keys. Words came next,
when he wanted a drink but forgot 'tea',
held up the queue at the station
trying to remember where he was going.
By the time he could not associate
the way he felt with the way to the bathroom
he'd lost the notion of embarrassment.
And then he asked his dearest granddaughter
who she was, what she was doing there.
We took that for 'Goodbye.'

MISSING PERSONS

Is it by chance, or elegant design
that hordes of people we don't know become
a momentary focus? Draw a line
round family and friends. A blurring thrum
of strangers smudges definition. There's
a jogger, passer-by, a man who sat
beside you on the bus, a plumber, nurse,
a waiter stopping for a friendly chat.
Each casual exchange adds to the store
of unacknowledged people we don't know
who've touched our lives an instant, gone before
we've noticed them arrive or watched them go.
Our world's reduced by almost-contacts, seen,
unregistered in realms of might-have-been.

BREAD

A day devoted to the bake of bread
begins in sanctity of strong white flour,
some ready yeast, coarse sea salt. Take a bowl
for mixing, kneading, resting. Sense by touch
if there's enough cool water. Let your hands
caress the first stir slowly. There is time

to relish scent and texture, for the time
between the baking and to eat the bread
should stretch like dough. You look down, see your hands
ingrained in white where powdered dust of flour

imprints your fingers, scatters at your touch
to form a snowy halo round the bowl.

Now, with magician's flourish, swathe the bowl
in cloth, and let the mixture take its time
to double up in size; and where its touch
has made your fingers sticky, feel how bread
will fill your mouth, your body. Grains of flour
are wiped away. And now it's in your hands,

the heritage, where generation hands
to generation, how this mixing bowl
is symbol of domestic arts that flower
in families, in friends, where sharing time
commands as much respect as sharing bread.
Communion takes place at handshake's touch.

The risen dough is ready for your touch.
You form it in a loaf shape with your hands,
and score the top, and place the unbaked bread
inside the hot, hot oven. Soak the bowl
before the washing up, and check the time.
No evidence remains – just dusted flour –

of all this ritual. You put the flour
away until next baking day. In touch
with elements of life, you sense how time
is slipping through your fingers. But your hands
have left their mark. In love, a simple bowl,
a cloth, and water all connect in bread.

The elements of flour and salt bless hands
that touch and clasp beneath the giant bowl
of sky, the stretch of time, the reach of bread.

SAFELY DELIVERED

Rebirthing began when he left,
when his three hundred pounds
rolled off her groaning chair
and mumbled oaths
as the grubby suitcase was packed.
She started with flowers,
a neat posy to change the air
to rosebuds, pot pourri for the bathroom.

Back at college, she aced
the physics he'd said she was too stupid
to learn, mastered the maths to work out
how many years and months,
weeks, days, hours and minutes
she had wasted on him.

On Saturdays she took the car
to the look-out where a panorama
gave misty mountains one way,
honey-coloured sand and rippling waves
the other. She could sit for three hours,
four, five, undisturbed,
deftly mixing oils to fill canvas after canvas
empty of all but possibilities.

Back home she tried nouvelle cuisine,
dined on an elegance of butter-soft steak,
asparagus, mushrooms,
no pile of fries in sight.

Friends came to visit again,
stirred by the twin excitements
of good conversation
and home made drop scones.

A year beyond his leaving
the papers arrived; and she wept
the awe, the joy, the sheer beauty
of safe delivery
after a long confinement.

NOT CRICKET

This sporting life is not the life for me.
The C-word sends a shudder through my bones.
I spend my match days buttering the scones.
I stay in the pavilion, make the tea.

The musty smell of kit and sweat set free
miasmas of revolting pheromones.
This sporting life is not the life for me,
the C-word sends a shudder. Through my bones,

my nerves, my muscles, sinews, lethargy
displaces boredom. Umpire's voice intones
'no-ball.' A non-event. In undertones
I moan of things I do for love ... you see
this sporting life is not the life for me.

TO THE NEXT GENERATION

I leave to you
my diamond rings, a first edition,
pictures of poppies and dandelions.
Worth more by far, I leave
my love of language, hope that you
will play with words,
tame them, befriend them.

I leave you the capacity
to see the sunny side,
to laugh easily, to stride your path
with confidence, this to compensate
for a lack of height,
excess of weight.

There will be things for you, cash, a home
(if they have not been squandered
by generations between)
and poems to surprise you,
worry you, please you.

I leave you no sporting prowess,
but dextrous fingers
to make and craft;
no singing voice, but an ear
to sense when notes are true.

I will not know you,
only hope some cosmic consciousness
alerts me to your presence,
you to mine. But know
although we shall never meet,
I send you love.

NEGATIVE

I fit the mask so tight pores cannot breathe
nor lips tremble, tears are dammed. Where freefall
of hair cascaded, a dark scarf wraps and tugs.

My clothes in monochrome kaleidoscope of grey
are blacked out by a dusty midnight cloak, swirling
earth into eddies of dirt, whipping wilderness in my wake.

My feet are bare, translucent skin
a dull bone blue, no telltale shoeprint to identify;
my heel and sole pass by without impression.

I have become a nothing person, shifting into shadows,
ghosts of memory shimmering in my head,
never letting a whisper betray me.

In this disguise I can creep through backcloths of time.
move unseen in your life's hidden corners. I
lean into your mind, learn to unravel you.

And with each passing moment
my nothingness increases, this negative of me
takes over, helps me to forget the self I was.

AT THE POETRY READING

Your words wait, poem by poem,
to thread through still air,
spill into the listeners' ears,
each a pearl of observation, layer on layer
smoothed in a perfect orb.

You stand before us, vulnerable,
exposing soul and self
while an audience shuffles, whispers,
laughs in the wrong places, coughs.

Each gem hangs a second,
echoes in consciousness, dissipates.

You are silent in the moment
where your lines are absorbed,
when minds grasp the rope
and test its pearl.

Applause knows the roar
of one hand clapping. People stand,
move to the bar,
seek reassurance in wine.

A twist of now severs every thread,
sends your poems rolling into dark corners
to melt into forgetting
like yesterday's dust.

INSTRUCTING THE ARTIST

No stuffy rooms and stuffy relatives –
paint me alone where wind whips marram grass,
sand pits my skin and waves gossip.
Let cornflower skies arc above me,
tinged with first lilac hints of twilight,
where seagulls flirt and float on thermals,
wheeling their wailing call.

Paint me in a robe of orange,
opulent, blaring its statement to the world,
shouting defiance that will not be silenced.

Paint me with a background of dove grey cliffs,
where black shadows invite with promises
of cooling dusk, anticipate a filigree
of seaweed, scrunch of shattered shells.

Paint a prowling cat beside me,
bewitched by the grains beneath its paws,
watching for a twitch of mice
to make the day ordinary; and let a shimmer
of flying fish freeze in mid-air the other side of me,
sharing strangeness of a new element.

Paint me with bold strokes, bigger than life,
louder than salt, greater than weeks
wasted in quiet and good manners and grey.

STAR OF THE SPRING
Sandro Botticelli

It took some time, I can tell you,
to place us all in the right poses,
with me as the focus, modest in pale blue,
hair chastely covered, hands elegantly splayed,
one on my wrap, one indicating
the route through Spring. For a moment
I thought the dark trees behind, the grey skies
were backing for a Madonna portrait,
not Venus time-fixed in April.

Flora grinned beside me, flaunting and flowery,
scattering early roses, trying to ignore
the lustful Zephyrus, nipping Chloris
with his shivery March winds. She,
barely covered, (emphasis on the 'bare'),
clearly hadn't thought how her surrender
would turn her from nymph into goddess.

And there, as ever, the gang of groupies
performed some mildly erotic dance moves,
each Grace graceless in – you've guessed it –
diaphanous veiling, accentuating
more than it hid. It's hard to say
if one (or all) had designs on Mercury,
but his gaze was all toward May,
his stance a perfect blend
of martial and effeminate.

So there we stood, hour on hour,
while Sandro fussed an angle here,
tweaked a veil there, fretted as we froze.
Even Florence is cold when your feet are naked.

He put the flight in later, lifting
Zephyrus from the ground, floating Cupid
above my head, reckless with blindfold and bow.

His flowers came later still, nearly two hundred,
most that experts could name; and those oranges
(a nod to the Medici) like globes
of golden light in black boughs.

For all the cold and cramps, I was glad
he'd picked me for his Venus. Artist's model
is not the highest calling in this life;
but I have an inkling my face
will be remembered for a few years.

DANTE'S DREAM

She gives meaning to love, meaning to life,
your Beatrice, and Love hovers
at the centre of it all, red lips kissing
her white waxen cheek, red wings furled,
blossoms and his golden arrow pointing at you.

Do you see red doves flying toward the tower
where passing bells toll? Do you see
the angels waiting to accompany her soul
to heaven? She lies swathed in silk,
the flaming hair you hardly dared to touch
tumbling over her shoulders, pillow splayed.

Poppies carpet the floor where you tread,
exude their scent of sleep,
and it seems you walk in a dreamstate,
Love taking your hand to warm hers
as it chills in death. And you
in black, head bowed,
cannot begin to imagine what happens next.

Her two handmaids wait
at her head and her feet, holding high
the veil with its scattered may
perfuming her final breath.
When they lower it, cover her face,
your last goodbye will be hushed.

There will be nothing left for you
but to write of heaven and hell,
the heaven of knowing her,
the hell of not. Your heart
will bleed through years, decades, centuries:
and because of you
hers will never be silenced.

THE SCAPEGOAT

I have stood before this painting many times,
imagined Holman Hunt
in all the fervour of a twenty-something
pushing back boundaries, travelling the Holy Land

in unholy conditions, finding his truth.

I have read Leviticus, wondered at laws
so foreign to today's beliefs, so stern.
I have longed to offload my sins, but
sage or sentimental, could never understand
why an innocent goat should carry them,
suffer starvation, bodily torture, die for me.

I half close my eyes, focus
on thoughts of treated canvas, brushes, pencils,
the warm, waxy smell of paint. I can hear
the swish of brush, feel the throb
of unremitting desert heat. Which did he prefer,
first painting or the larger one, the second,
rainbow's promise gone, the goat
more white, more vulnerable?

How did he feel, binding red to wrap its horns
to symbolise its burden of sin? How did he feel
when his model fell, exhausted, overexposed,
with or without sin? From the vast and vicious
expanse of the Dead Sea background
to added details in a London studio,
how did his scapegoat haunt him?

Did he imagine how one
born a hundred years after his painting,
living a hundred years after his death,
could stand before his picture
in all the cynicism of a sixty-something
and weep?

THE ANNUNCIATION
Fra Angelico

She had to be at prayer, this Mary.
For monastery walls it would not be fitting
to see her at household tasks,
or carrying water, talking with other girls
in small-town Nazareth. No,
her stool and prayerbook prove the praying,
the vaulted passage walled, floored, roofed
in marble, arches bathed in lambent light
glowing around Gabriel, shadowed over her.

She clasps the open book,
unsubtle metaphor to show
she is open to whatever strange quest
is visited upon her; clutches
cascading folds of her robe
to feel the familiar of its fabric.

She cannot – dare not – meet the angel's gaze,
as if his eyes can penetrate
too far into her soul. Instead
she fixes her focus
on sturdy wings, a mass of peach down
giving way to ranks of blood red,
mourning grey on black,
tight furls whose freeing will beat a path
back to heaven.

His face is gentle, arms
reflecting hers
crossed in anticipation of first caress
of a new-born child, held
against a red-gold wrapped breast.

Just beyond the colonnade,
eclipsed by the archangel,
St. Peter the Martyr prays.
Upright, head slightly bowed in deference,
he remains a presence
but on the periphery, a Joseph in waiting.

All is static. All is calm.
Only a trinity of haloes suggests
circles of life, obedience, service;
that something is about
to be completed.

HAIKU

April's dawn chorus
sweetens a new day rising;
breathes earth's fresh promise.

FOCUS

It snowed all night, not polite snow,
a self-effacing blanket, but a blizzard
blotting out the moon, driving packed walls of white
to re-make road and hedge, last eddies
drifting their final coat of frosting.

Waking to new blue light
sharpened vision. To scoop a ball of snow
showed every flake's planes and angles,
sparking different shades
before they were compacted into rock
that fossilized each fingerprint's impression.

Where a fox had walked,
paws' indentations showed the pressure
on every pad. A crow slicing sky
left trails of black dust from its wings
sifting through brittle air.

Pale sun refracted in a spectrum,
glittered colours never seen before,
created hard edges to the muffled sheep,
each fibre of fleece distinct.

Breathing in was laboured, breathing out
a mist displacing morning's starkness,
breaking silence as its droplets disturbed.

There will be thaw, a dumbing down
of brilliance, landscape merging and blurring:
but a recollection of such clarity changes
how the mind's eye sees, focuses, remembers -
cannot be extinguished.

A JOB WORTH DOING ...

There he is, outside the back of the club,
in his shirtsleeves in breath-freeze cold,
sucking hard to catch a cigarette's last comfort
before his fingers burn, and muttering.
Get closer. Listen. He's telling a joke,
trying a gag over and over, hearing its tempo,
testing its pauses, estimating whether 'garden' or 'yard'
is funnier. He slides back round the door.
Follow him to his 'dressing room', curtained corner
with table, chair, mirror. He riffs fingers through his hair,
grimaces, makes his stage face, finds an energy
to bound in front of the audience, begin his barrage of patter.

There he is, outside the back of the club,
a wad of notes warming his pocket, clambering
into the groaning car, laughter ricocheting around.
Drained, he drives familiar roads, his mind concentrating
on how to tighten a flabby phrase, angle his head
to signpost a gag more neatly. Fatigued, exhausted,
he counts down miles to a lonely beer and bed.

There they are, his audience,
leaving the club on a high, reminding each other
of this joke, that - all a little brighter
for a night of silliness and laughter, fun,
an ignore-your-troubles night, a night
when for an hour or two, everything has seemed
a little better, a bit more positive, tinged
with light to lift spirits, the relief of forgetting,
an unexpected route to hope.

31st DECEMBER, 1799

See where they stand beside the lake, the man
all muffled up against the cold crisp air,
his sister swathed in shawls, and hear them plan
a new life in their new home. See them there,
at Grasmere's edge, where dusk has redefined
the hills beyond. This water, deep and dark,
is shifting Muse to move his restless mind,
to fill his pen with magic, kindle sparks
of poetry. As night turns grey to black
and moon rise draws its silver streak, both know
this place will seed their future, don't look back,
but plot the journey their twinned lives will go.
    And as they watch, a million stars, fluorescing
    on lake's still surface, echo water's blessing.

READING CORNERED

It began in childhood, characters
rising from my favourite books
to talk to me, play with me.
I welcomed them, shared honey
with a small, golden bear, apples
as Jim Hawkins told his tales
of almost-empty islands. Still learning
to separate real from dreams, I guessed
it was the same for everyone.

When Alice took my hand
and let me fall with her
into her other world, I wondered;
but schooldays grounded me
and rabbit holes became
the ankle-wrenching boobytraps
we all avoided.

The edges of my worlds blurred
when I met Cathy on one bleak windswept walk,
and she poured out her confusion
in the wailing twilight. For hours
my arm felt chilled
where she had touched me, my lips
blue-grey as dark Yorkshire stone.

Then the fear started. Clanking
of Marley's chains clattered in my head,
and a stench of death clogged my throat.
Mary Shelley's monster lurched at me
and kept coming. Birds flocked
from du Maurier pages, wheeled and cried,
then darted at me,
claws scratching, beaks stabbing.

Now I am afraid to breathe, stir, show my presence.
They are all lined up, Christie's poisoners,
Lee Child's sadists, Bond villains,
all putting me in terror of a head-on meeting;
all putting me in terror of turning the page.

MISS S. PAYS A VISIT

I have been here a hundred times,
paced in tasteful awe
these parquet floors,
tiled kitchens, cobbled yards,
wondered at antique oak furniture,
towering fireplaces.

Today there is no need to draw down blinds.
A petulant sun peeped once, withdrew,
and sulks in cloud. A grandfather clock
shares his ennui in every tick. But listening
beyond the wheezing groans
of ancient heaters, I can hear the plod
of heavy boots moving closer, lighter footsteps
swishing and flirting down corridors,
ghosts or imagination's tricks.

Darkness rolls through the ballroom,
and I see I'm on my own here,
no guides, no other visitors;
and yet I sense that someone watches, feel
warm breath stir the hairs on my neck, smell
a hint of lilacs. As I turn, a peacock blue gown
teases peripheral vision. Before I can spin back,
invisible hands slip the rope around my neck.

One crack of pain and I am slipping
through my mind, losing
all I know of time elapsing,
of hunger, heat and cold, the need to sleep.

I have been here a hundred times,
and now I know I can stay
surrounded by friends, the Colonel, Professor,
Vicar and the Cook,
all drifting in and out of these rooms,
urging lead piping, a gun,
a candlestick into my hands,
promising a future where life is a game.

(Please note that Miss S. has absolutely no interest in female toxicologists, baseball bats, axes, etc.)

HAIKU

March: tadpoles wriggle
from spawn to bud, embody
a promise of frogs.

'ONE OF THE FINEST'
(Martin Luther King Jr. of Rosa Parks)

It was the bus that started it,
the daily walk to school, overtaken
by smugly seated white kids riding to theirs.
Some things are not the same.

She never forgot the day she queued,
boarded the bus, paid – was ordered off
for walking to her seat, told to re-board
at the rear door. She recalls
how the driver's grim smile gleamed
as he sped past, left her on the pavement.

Chance saw the driver, twelve years on,
insist she yield her place
so a white man shouldn't stand.
She sat, remained until police were called,
endured humiliation of arrest.

A perfect scapegoat, demure seamstress,
married, dignified ... ticked boxes turned tides.
Her guilty verdict was appealed,
segregation challenged, catalyst to a grapevined boycott.
Forty thousand walked, took cabs, shared cars
for a day, a year, then more
while buses stood idle.

A hero by default, but moved on
once too often, Rosa lit the torch
to spark a brighter future, brought redress
for every Jim Crow victim of the past.

MARBLE

Our blue marble rolls
around its prescribed course,
whirls and spins while we are fixed
atom small, rooted in our infinitesimal fragment.
Safely cocooned,
we know nothing of fragility,
scarcely guess the ease of shattering
if the marble should implode.

We are told
of changing climates, plastic detritus,
fossil fuel, waste,
but sense our microscopic lives
are too insignificant to matter.

With quiet desperation
we accept impotence, only need
a visionary glimpse to gather
how each minute act
of conservation, preservation,
upcycling, repurposing, caring,
keeps the marble rolling.

THIS IS JUST TO SAY ...

Dear Walt

Was it your idea to translate
vers libre into our idiom?
Or was it simply
that you were the best
of your generation?
Did you free the mind
of frustration and fetters
to compensate where emotion
was in chains? Could you know
the glory of your quiet revolution?

A century and a half passed
between your birth and my finding you,
and in that time
your innovation progressed
from quirk to norm,
from staggering to unremarkable.

Your vision has touched
seasoned cynic, embryo experimenter,
provided a springboard
to make poems soar, a cushion
for their landing, a bedrock
for the coming generations.
Thank you.

       Sincerely

          A. Poet

TABLE FOR TWO

We went for the pasta,
light, finely herbed, flaked with salmon;
stayed for the music. For when he played,
that tall man with the salt-and-pepper beard,
he conjured youth we had forgotten.

With that trick of memory, forgetting yesterday,
recalling fifty years ago, we joined in,
sang all the words sotto voce,
to Gerry's Ferry 'Cross the Mersey,
wished with the Beach Boys
that all could be California Girls,
Painted it Black with the Rolling Stones.

Between songs we reminisced,
snatches of moments with a background
of Herman's Hermits, Simon and Garfunkel,
and we laughed remembering Monkee antics
harmonising Saturday teatime.

A bottle of cava later, volume increased.
We joined Cliff on his Summer Holiday –
glanced a little shamefaced at the next table;
saw they were singing to Now or Never,
and Elvis, Hollies, Kinks, Mamas and Papas
turned the restaurant to one luscious, food-filled karaoke.

Beatles came with the bill. Everyone chanted
the Yellow Submarine, revelled in the Octopus's Garden,
declared She Loves You, grieved for Yesterday.
And singing with that blackbird in the dead of night,
we walked in unison into warm dark,
your voice melting over me: P.S. I Love You.

LONDON, 1665

Your head is filled with horrors. Naked fear
pervades your dreams by night, your thoughts by day.
You're watching for some symptom to appear,
know headache, vomit, fever pave the way
to black, necrotic swellings, know that they
could toll your death knell. And you understand
your neighbours, townsfolk share your grim dismay,
and panic spreads like plague across the land.

Nobody seems to know the cause. You hear
that smoke and heat will clean the air. They say
to sniff a sponge of vinegar will clear
impurities. Applying leeches may
remove infection with the blood. Decay
is all around you, and on every hand
black rats are scavenging, the dead their prey,
and panic spreads like plague across the land.

All thoughts of hope and comfort disappear.
You can't recall the joys of yesterday.
Imagination stifles. You can't steer
your mind to any other track. To stay
means almost certain death; to run away
the same. You're dicing with the devil ... and
his dice are loaded. You've no choice. You play,
and panic spreads like plague across the land.

Your world has changed forever, and today
disease has burned its message in a brand
that's scorched the future unremitting grey;
and panic spreads like plague across the land.

LONDON, 2020

                        31st December
Dear Diary …
It came by stealth, this unseen enemy,
scaled the walls of the whole world
while we, safe in our British stoicism,
bickered and laughed, shopped, walked the dog,
worried at the ordinary.

We lost a year, lost our liberty
to the invader, lost so many precious souls;
saw sickness lay waste,
funerals bereft of mourners,
empty, masked weddings.

But we have found a hoard of goodness,
of hidden strengths that prompt
people to give when an old man walks,
a footballer who won't see children starve,
a million acts of kindness
that have the power to heal.

And as the year turns into '21,
we re-learn hope in phalanxes of vials
whose frozen secret is our lethal weapon.
We shall re-learn to shed the fear,
embrace our friends, unite
to laugh and celebrate in public spaces.

We shall carry this season's blessings
to warm first hints of spring,
free summer from its fetters,
turn our desperate weeping
into tears of joy.

IDYLL

All is still in the garden.
No breeze moves a blade of grass
in its emerald carpet. In dawn's newness,
buds are starting to show colour,
white apple blossom froths on boughs,
laurels shine, marigolds
are opening to entice early bees.

A thrush tries
his first hesitant trill, another,
then a cascade of song
bursts from his throat. Butterflies
flicker through honey-sweet air,
and a snail edges up a rose's thorny stem.

Just one tree already glows with fruits
more rich and rare
than any in the garden. In a niche
between its roots, a knotted serpent sleeps.

There's a single empty space
in this divine setting; a gap
to be filled by a man, a woman.
Then this strange, wild experiment
can begin.

LATE FLIGHT

It was in that dead time,
eulogies over, prayers prayed;
we shivered in bright colours as requested,
looked uncertainly toward the cosy of cars.

In the bowels of the brick slab of building
engineers did what they must
to render dust to ashes. Overhead
in a cloudless, duckegg blue sky,
wave after wave of geese
veed across limitless space.

Those great arrows
etched magic into air,
swooped and swept in swathes
calling their whooping cry.

And we
who knew our dear friend's love
for every bird in the heavens,
smiled for the first time that day,
reassured by the certainty
that they were carrying her home.

BALANCING ACT

You fear the camera. Its image takes
a fraction of your soul – locks it away
so part of you's fragmented. If it makes
your spirit scatter, what fine interplay
can link your essence with the now of you,
bind past and future with your presence here?
One photograph secures one moment. Who
can work out when your soul will disappear,
displaced to petrify while you live on,
diminished and shell-brittle? Hide your eyes,
your face, and it's intact; but when you're gone
there will be nothing left to recognise.
    So trade your image for a shred of soul.
    Part icon and part spirit make one whole.

STUMBLE

It started as a stumble.
I fumbled footing, fell backwards
into that shallow pool in rock
within the cool, deep cave.

Shock of water was ice cold,
despite the heat outside. I gasped,
struggled, tried to stand,
free myself of the coffin-shaped dip.

But even as other visitors crowded,
reached hands to help me,
tissues to wipe my salt-smeared face,
I realised I had no desire to move.

I could spend my life here,
warm breezes and the drift of brine
at the cave's entrance, pebbles
swirled smooth by millennia of tides.

The going back would bring
ordinary problems, day by dry day.
Here I could lie till brackish water
evaporated, crisping like stranded seaweed.

Alerted by the group who'd tried to help,
my friends, ahead, exploring the next cave,
came back, hauled me up, laughed
as embarrassment reddened.

They brought me home,
embellished tales of my soaking, my escape,
gave me back to ordinary problems
day by dry day.

And often I retrace the cliff path,
wish tides in and out, feel texture
of shells in my hand, rock at my back,
wish for the halflife of stranded seaweed.

MY MOST DEAR LORD, KING AND HUSBAND

It was the hardest letter
I have ever had to write, and now,
exhausted, weakened as I am,
to read it through stirs deepest pain.

I had the best of Henry, so young,
so tall and strong, so beautiful. I used
all the words my new language gave,
none of the stilted Latin
I had shared with Arthur. I remember
the words he returned, the poems,
his dear voice singing music
of his own invention.

I remember the grief and desperation on his face
when one child died, the next, the next,
and five pairs of eyes closed
in forever sleep. For him, survival
of a mere girl was nature's final slap.

Yet even when I knew
his glance had fallen on that Boleyn witch,
young enough to be my child,
I would never, could never
stop loving him.

Today I felt a need, an urgency
to write that letter. I am more frail
each passing day, I see my body
turn to bone, not only from the fasting.

I had to plead
his love for our dear Mary, his care
that my servants should have money:
I had to tell him
I forgive, although forgiveness
was not sought,
but I must cleanse my soul
before my body can unleash it.

I had to close
by telling him once more
that all my love, all my desire
are only his.

The lights are dimming.
Whether I am sick or poisoned,
I know I will not be here long,
my time measured in days, not months.

The letter will remain.
He will read it. He will keep it.
He will know.

(Shortly before her death, Catherine of Aragon, widow of Prince Arthur and first wife of Henry VIII, wrote a highly emotional letter to Henry, commencing with the words of the title).

RAIN DANCE

We danced barefoot the day it rained,
    a joyous tread
        measured on hard packed earth.

First slow drops
    settled like oil in globules
        now penetrating the ground.

As drips turned to deluge
    and we could breathe again,
        we raised drenched faces to cloud.

Soil yielded and plumped,
    mud oozed between our toes,
        and every leaf knew blessing.

It has been a month now.
    The rain has not stopped.
        Roads are rivers.

Foundations awash, our home
    is foundering, will implode; and we
        shall not dance, but drown.

GARDENER

Each day he tends their garden, too aware
she'd scold at any untrimmed blade of grass,
dead rose heads, clematis that's climbed too far.

Each afternoon at four he makes a drink,
puts china cups and saucers on a tray,
pours milk, pours tea, finds book and newspaper.

Each evening he works, ignores her, makes
a meal, makes conversation while she sings
diminuendo as the shadows fall.

He showers and cleans his teeth, turns down the bed,
unfolds crisp-ironed pyjamas, puts them on.
To turn the light off means that he can hear

the whisper of her breathing in the dark,
hypnotic, lulling him to fall asleep.
He wakes at two, bathed in congealing sweat.

Each night his nightmares are the same, disturb
with images of decomposing flesh,
a stench he tastes, the jar of every thud

his golf club sounded as it met her skull.
By now she will be nothing more than bone.
Perhaps he'll dig the flowerbeds, making sure.

Each morning, as he turns off the alarm,
he gazes at the far side of the bed
and murmurs *Morning, Darling, nearly eight.*

There's no more nagging, snide remarks, complaints,
no barked instructions, shrill and shrewish rants.
Each day he tends the garden, and he smiles.

JULY NIGHT

He slept outside that night,
lay on an ill-sprung garden lounger
languishing under brighter stars than he'd ever seen
in the deepest blueblack sky he'd even known
the hottest summer in memory.

She lay in an ill-sprung hospital bed
leaning across to touch the perspex box
where their future stirred in first sleep.

He was woken by insistent images
of helplessness, doing nothing but holding her hand,
hating to hear every gasp and pain-filled cry.

She could still feel the imprint
of his strong hand holding hers, marvel
at his calm, mesmerised by the sight of him
holding the child as though
he had held her for all of his life.

Three thirty. Five hours old.
She opened sapphire eyes,
began to learn night heat,
the cool of cotton,
her mother's breath from the outside.

From a first piping whistle,
a dawn chorus, louder than there'd ever been,
tuned up, blasted a cacophony
of celebration, congratulation,
songs and calls mingling, crescendoing,
welcoming the dawn
of their changed world.

THE HAND THAT ROCKS THE CRADLE

I watch my daughter playing trains with her son,
suckling her baby girl; see past her tiredness
to the inner glow that fuels
her magic kisses on a bruised knee,
the knowledge that even the most health-conscious parents
need to know when chocolate's required,
her understanding that bedtimes may be fluid.

I wonder at her wisdom
making good manners a game, not a lesson,
her imagination to conjure bedtime stories
relevant to each day's lows and highs,
her patience with persistent questions
and how-far-dare-I-go mischief.

I do not know what instinct
taught her everything she didn't learn from me,
transformed my muddling through
into a tide of getting it right,
wave on wave of fun balanced with common sense,
every day an experience, an opportunity.

I only know the next generation
is in safer hands than the last.

ENDURANCE

I didn't sign up for this, the Endurance
off to the bitter reaches of Antarctica.
Twenty-seven of us, there were. No, twenty-eight,
(an idiot stowed away) and all those dogs,
a cat to catch the rats.

It only took two days, and we hit
thick ice around the continent. We laboured on.
A month into the voyage we were stuck fast.
Gale forced, hard packed ice trapped us.
For Tommy we were 'frozen like an almond
in the middle of a chocolate bar'.

For a full nine months we festered there,
the cold impossible, food worse,
company worse still. And nothing to do but wait.

We shot the animals, grabbed what we could
of food and ropes, tools and bibles,
clothes and personal treasures. At least
someone thought to bring three lifeboats.

She sank a few weeks later: we noted her position
then set out to march over the ice.
A week took us seven miles. We camped for months,
and when the ice broke up, set off
to row the lifeboats to Elephant Island.
Most of the men were sick, exhausted,
convulsed with dysentery. Half were mad.

Some died, some survived. Shackleton lived
to die another day, on another expedition.
The dice rolled my way. I went home,
spent the rest of my days on dry land.

Endurance? They've found her, salted and silted
on the ocean bed. There she'll stay, in company
with ghosts of sailors she couldn't kill,
the eerie bark of dogs and call of cat.

OUTSIDER

It's cold outside. Wind-chilled and frosty air
invades your chest, and breathing hurts. Nowhere
gives shelter, and the ceaseless storm of hail
soaks through your clothes. Thin blood turns you snow-pale,
and you find no relief or help out there.

You stumble to a doorway, crouch down, stare
across the web of years, across the square.
Fierce coughing jars your frame: lungs start to fail.
                    It's cold outside.

Eons ago, you had a wife, a pair
of red-cheeked children laughing, playing where
you lived and worked and loved. But love grew stale;
you fought, you lost. Fate drove the final nail.
You walk the streets. There's no one left to care.
                    It's cold outside.

A PRESENT FROM MOSTYN

The battered cardboard box
travelled further than she ever had,
brought to me when my great aunt died.

Newspapers protecting its contents
crumbled, brittle with age. I reached in,
brought out a mirror in a wooden frame,

surprised she should have owned
this symbol of vanity, that maiden lady
severe in black, unsmiling, starched and prim.

Her bible was there, minus its cover,
thumbed and scuffed from reading beside the oil lamp
in a power-less, running-water-less Welsh cottage.

There was a cheap glass vase,
though I doubted anybody gave her flowers,
and a white china cup.

Not much to show for a life.
Not much of a life; but as I touched her things,
collapsed that sad cardboard box,

remembered her severity, my fear
on those rare visits, I found myself hoping
she had known a sort of happiness.

FAMILY FEUD

'Rules made must not be broken,' Father warned.
'One rule is sacrosanct. No Capulet
May ever enter here,' I was informed.
Except for playing devil's advocate
Out of a teen compulsion to rebel,
My will concurred with his. Our enmity,
Age old, (the cause forgotten, truth to tell),
Did not affect me much. Heredity
Ordained I had no wish to break his rule.
Remember, though, my gang and I were thrashed,
Each full of cheap rough wine, and out to fool
Sad old man Capulet. So we gatecrashed.
Juliet smiled. She spoke. And I was lost,
Consumed by love, impossibly star-crossed.

Just when I thought this party was the dross,
Useless, pathetic, there he stood. It cost
Little to smile and say hello. Half smashed,
(I'd sneaked a cup of brandy), I felt cruel
Enough to lead him on, so, unabashed,
Trying to hide a laugh, I let him drool.
Can you imagine how it turned on me
As he responded, and my rogue heart fell
Down to an unplumbed depth of love? You see,
Our tenet – Death to Montagues – might well
Result in my death, too; for when we met
Each fibre of me throbbed with longing, formed
So strongly, I would die for him. We let
Rules shatter. And my being was transformed.

THE ARTIST'S BEDROOM, 1889

So what do I expect
of an artist's bedroom? A few stray brushes?
A mural of a night sky, all stars and swirls?
Portrait with a prominent ear?
A paint stained dressing gown?
Certainly not all this unremitting blue.

Was it meant to calm your disquiet,
bring peace to the chaos of your imagining?
Did it merely deepen
the depths of your misery?

The blue of walls renders
the window's light cheerless.
The blue of door saps appearance of warmth
from a red quilt. Blue jackets hang
near nondescript pictures. A blue bowl and jug
suggest tepid water for washing.

Perspective narrows this cell,
coffin cold, its only comfort
two rattan chairs. Square table and solid bed
are diminished into the distance.

Would it have hurt to add
boughs of almond blossoms, a bunch
of iris, twelve sunflowers in a vase?
Could that chair beside the bed
have held a bottle of absinthe and a pipe?

I wish I could have been let loose
on that room, Vincent, with a pot of yellow,
a bright crocheted coverlet,
a hooked rag rug, a scarlet smoking jacket.
I wish I could have brought rosy light
to shine away your shadows.

SEA DANCE

I want a part in Vettriano's 'The Singing Butler',
wearing a sheath-thin satin dress, daring bare feet.
I want to dance where wavelets tease the shore,
where watchers bend and shiver under umbrellas.

Wearing a sheath-thin satin dress, daring bare feet
beside your ballroom shoes, I long to feel warm
fingers on my back, your strong arms leading me.

I want to dance where wavelets tease the shore,
feel our foxtrot glide to the butler's silent singing,
ignore heavy, windblown raindrops falling

where watchers bend and shiver under umbrellas.
I want us to dance till sun sets under grey clouds,
to say I love you all the long drive home.

STURNUS VULGARIS
(Common Starling)

You hardly see them on the salt marsh,
where sand, rough grass and puddles pit earth,
and they are camouflaged, brown-feathered,
flashed with green and purple.

Get closer, and you hear the starlings call,
their own songs interspersed
with clicks and whistles, tweets and burs,
mimics of cellphone, siren, other birds.

The show begins when the murmuration rises,
bird on bird, ten starlings, a hundred, a thousand,
more, creating a ballet so graceful,
so perfectly choreographed,

a human dancer would weep
to have such beauty. They whirl and spin,
reel, curve in complex spirals, swoop,
ascend, drop back to swirl upwards again.

They may be being chased,
each tiny heart thudding, each breast
panicked by approaching raptors. Or they may
be revelling in light's ebb and flow.

By instinct or instinctive calculation,
each bird moves with the seven in its sight,
aware of its place in teeming multitudes,
aware of space above, below, around.

With the same suddenness that started
this strange ballet, bird on bird descends
back to the ordinariness of ground,
back to shiny-feathered anonymity.

HERITAGE

I was born where, five thousand years ago,
Neolithic man carved shapes and symbols
into the Calder Stones to line a chambered tomb –
a bird, a snake, a spiral – and sandstone grit
mixed with the dust of bones
of my forefathers.

Air I breathe today
was inhaled, exhaled by monks who rowed the ferry
eight hundred years before I knew this water,
crossing where Irish Sea and River Mersey mingle.

In Saint George's Hall Dickens' readings,
Victoria's approval reverberate with echoes
of pleas and verdicts, sentences given,
music from the massive organ's seven thousand pipes,
a hundred years before my birth.

And from forever, for forever,
the city inspires musicians and artists,
poets, philosophers and politicians,
inventors, dancers and comedians
all sharing one proud heritage:
Made in Liverpool.

COLD

It is so cold today I cannot stop
the ice from forming deep in my body.

Bone brittles where its marrow solidifies.
Blood is crisp red flakes frosting veins,
freezing my heart's beat to a silent shudder.
Fingers fuse where skin adheres to skin
and toes snap under pressure.

My brain directs its last coherent thought
to memories of heat, days stretched in sun,
nights of wine and dance, and then ...

THE CLASS FAILURE

We were the Chosen Ones,
plucked from anonymity in classes of clones
to be fast-tracked, hoisted
into Academia. Fifteen of our number
were earmarked for excellence from the start.
I, the sixteenth, happened to get good marks
in English, French, Mathematics.
I flew on their coat-tails.

They ascended, emerged from the bottle-green chrysalis
to top their year at Oxford, read Latin or Law,
become politicians, doctors, captains of industry
before glass ceilings were conceived.
I was quite good at drama,
but never had a part in the School Play.

Through time's passage and house moves we lost touch.
The rest were fixed as the fifteen,
beside five hundred others and me,
grouped around a phalanx of seated teachers
in the long scroll of a school photograph.

When we were forty, one of the Successes
suggested a reunion. We met
over a beige buffet in a large hotel,
ate pies and sandwiches, cocktail sausages,
vol-au-vents, like at those birthday parties
so many years before. We shared

how this marriage had failed,
that career had foundered,
the years of unsuccessful fertility treatment,
the illnesses and angst.

I thought my thankfulness
for half a lifetime's love with the same husband,
two beautiful daughters, a portfolio career
where everything I did made me happy,
and kept my mouth shut.

RAINED OFF

I wandered through a mist-soaked cloud
that hovered low among the trees;
saw visitors in gloomy crowds
complaining that a gentle breeze
had changed to squall and drenching storm.
They longed to be back home and warm.

They'd come to see the daffodils
but cold, wet March dictated just
the odd sad straggly flower. The hills
were soggy quagmires. Every gust
of bitter wind shook trees, churned lakes,
and made them yearn for tea and cakes.

For England's North West corner boasts
nice views, but every day it rains,
and while, in theory, golden hosts
of daffodils are worth the pains
of cold and wet, in fact it's mad
to think those weeds make dull hearts glad.

And often, when I'm feeling blue,
and thoughts are vacant, glum and flat,
I find a helpful thing to do
is revel in the knowing that
things could be worse. At least I'm not
in that grim, flowerless, sodden spot.

Please note that any 'down' on the Lake District has been grossly exaggerated. The same applies to Yorkshire, but balance requires a response ...

DAY TRIP TO HALIFAX

It was a special, secret joy, that 'cheap day' ticket,
gift for friends and family to ride the rails
for peppercorn payment. Manchester always came first,
and we climbed down from oily carriages to stand
in indecision on a draughty platform.

The Middle of England spread itself like El Dorado,
each glittering destination tempting Pick me! Pick me!
Leeds offered bits we'd missed last time,
Buxton sat upright in Victorian rectitude,
Huddersfield reminded their station was spectacular.
Halifax was unexplored. We boarded the train.

A long chug down the line, and Lancashire's cotton mills
yielded to Yorkshire wool. Eager to explore, we hurried
to find the nearest point of interest.
The Tourist Information officer seemed surprised
to be disturbed, but he offered:
The Piece Hall. It was shut – no trade there.
Industrial Museum. It was shut – out of order.
Minster. It was shut – no prayers ascending to heaven today.

A short walk away, we found a mill turned Art Gallery,
a Shopping Mall, and a smiling soft-spoken man who,
with a friend, was building a perfect replica of the place in lego.

We spoke little on our way back to the train,
just remarked that the stained glass market ceiling was stunning,
even though stalls were sparse.

Manchester buzzed with excited crowds, its station
bursting with bustle and trains. We changed lines for home,
smuggled a bottle of wine into the dry carriage.
It was scant compensation for Halifax.

REJECTED

I am thinking of complaining
to the shop. I lost my heart
to this rather gorgeous biro -
quite expensive, very smart.

I bought it, wrote a sonnet,
but its vague attempts at rhyme
and its dodgy, rough pentameters
made this a waste of time.

I chanced it on a villanelle,
but at the third repeat
it made a blot and lost the plot
and dropped the metric beat.

It nearly caught a limerick,
but just before the end
it ran out of all the funny.
Then things started to descend.

It inserted an expletive
in a neatly worked pantoum,
and it placed a rogue apostrophe,
it really made me fume.

It muddled a sestina.
This has really got to stop.
Tomorrow I'm returning it,
rejected, to the shop.

BALLROOM REVISITED

Oh, those stolen hours long ago,
when we were young and lithe,
when pressing my body to yours
made foreplay of a waltz,
when the swinging hips
made one-two-cha-cha-cha
raw sex on the dancefloor.
How I would love to recapture them.

The chance came: a church hall
swaying to Marimba Rhythm
at ten thirty in the morning,
and a dozen couples
of eyewatering average age
struggled to follow instructions,
then struggled to remember them
five minutes later.

I pressed expanded girth into you,
felt you wince as your knees locked,
made one-two-cha-cha-cha
the rhythm of gentle exercise
for the over seventies.
But it was worth the agony
of new shoes, the grate of old hips,
the pain in linked fingers,
to look into your eyes
and see the same twinkle.

MIRROR IMAGE

It was looking into a mirror
and seeing no reflection
that convinced me. Even then
I could not quite believe I was dead.

I could feel the weight of my body
pressing in on me, the ground
beneath my feet, a cool breeze
chilling my face, the face I knew was there
but the mirror did not.

I tried to put my arms
around my husband, tell him
there was no need for that silent sobbing.
He shivered, dissolved beneath my touch.

I stared into the picture frame,
the one that always mocked when I dusted,
my features, dim in its glass, aging year on year,
my photo fixed at thirty.
Only the photo looked back.

No glimmer of me ghosted
the patio door. No shadow
blurred the shiny bathroom tiles.

I shall stand before this mirror
for an hour. For eternity.
If I try hard enough,
I might find myself.

SPACE INVADER

Here, in a cactus garden
of spikes, squat palms,
set among stone chippings,
lies an interloper.
Smoothly swollen, purple, sensual,
a single eggplant reclines,
deeply bedded in grey.

Its presence flaunts, unexplained.
It could have made a bid for escape
from a band of vegetables
secured in a shopping bag;
but who would walk their shopping
through this tourist-haven garden?
It could have been hurled at a carnivore
by an angry mob of vegetarians,
but has sustained no bruising.
It could have materialised out of empty air,
but that seems unlikely.

It gleams, smugly hugging its secret cache
of fibre, potassium, vitamins, minerals,
at the same time hoarding its toxic load
of nightshade alkaloids.

There will be, no doubt,
a logical explanation
for its disconcerting presence;
but here, in the cactus garden,
only one thing is sure.
Somebody, somewhere,
is one aubergine
short of a moussaka.

EYE TO EYE

I swim from shore to this rocky outcrop,
find myself face to face, eye to eye
with a dozen huge crabs,
Grapsus Adscensionis, Sally Lightfoot.
Each spares a glance, then stares, unshifting,
fixes me with a curious gaze
as if it can't quite believe.

I search to dredge from memory decapod,
arthropod, crustacea; wonder
with an artist's eye, at olive, teal, bottle green
for its carapace; fire, scarlet for those legs,
those pincers. Quick as winking

one sidesteps off the rock, slides
beside me in the water, vanishes.
I peer through green mist,
strain to catch sight of my harlequin friend.

His fellows join a fishy game
of follow-my-leader, sink
to spread the sea-bed word
of un-shelled pink invading their basking.

I swim back to shore, gladdened by motley,
count myself companion to a cast of crabs
who have let me share their time, their space.

AFTER THE DINOSAURS

It starts with microbes, algae, water fleas
that teem in oceans, slither onto sand
as fish emerging from primeval seas.

Yet breathing air, and feeling rain, the breeze,
sun's heat, all make it hard to understand
it starts with microbes. Algae, water fleas,

and starfish, sharks and tuna, squid and eels
will morph to mammals, reptiles, birds, new planned
as fish emerging from primeval seas

begin to change, re-shape our world. So bees
and butterflies, a million species: and …
it starts. With microbes, algae, water fleas,

a wild explosion thunders. Now the seeds
of new life are dispersed, which owe their brand
to fish emerging from primeval seas.

This fresh beginning, re-birth, sweet reprise
crescendoes, sending shock waves through the land.
It starts with microbes, algae, water fleas,
and fish emerging from primeval seas.

UNINVITED GUEST

Believing I was alone, I felt my heart quicken
to the sound of rustling, scratching,
a tiny sigh. When no-one answered
to my call of 'Anybody there?'
I guessed imagination had been stirred.
The sounds continued.

By now I knew the perpetrator
must be smaller than I, more timid than I.
I braved each nook, each cranny of the kitchen -
traced sounds to a corner. There he was,
a small dome of prickles burrowing at my wall.

I watched a full five minutes,
saw tiny paws rummaging,
breaking fragile plaster as he hunted
for whatever he believed thrived there.

Each separate spine rippled
as he moved, black button nose snuffling,
that little body a concertina
extending, contracting as he worked.

He was so intent on his task,
my movement did not disturb him.
I ripped open a pack of the cat's meat,
mashed it down in a saucer.
He took it as his due.

He came again, many times. We left his saucer
just outside, watched his arrivals and departures
from the kitchen window. Sometimes
he looked up. I like to think he smiled.

One day he proved our assumption was wrong.
She brought three hoglets
to share her feast; told them, I hope,
the kitchen walls harboured
no slugs or grubs; told them, I hope,
there was a welcome here.

ODYSSEUS TAKES THE SCENIC ROUTE

Picture this: you've been at war ten years
fighting Trojans. You've won. The journey home
should be a celebration. At first it's going well.
You stop at Ismaros for food and water; grab
gold as well. The gods are not amused.

You reach another island. Your hosts,
hospitable, give your men lotus nectar.
It makes them lose their desire for home.
You have to strongarm them back to the boat.

On the island of the Cyclops, giant Polyphemus
eats some of your men. You blind him ... that
annoys his father who happens to be Poseidon.
You still have friends in high places.
At your next stop, Aeolus, wind god, gives you
a bag full of west winds to open at home. Your men,
curious, open it ... and the journey gets longer.

After the storm, you fetch up on Telepylos.
Its king eats your landing party, while his men
smash up eleven ships and start on the crew.
You row fast. Aeaea, next port of call, is home
to the sorceress Circe, who turns your crew
into pigs, and keeps them for a year.

Not a good party. You make the Underworld
your next stop, hoping Tiresias can point you
towards Ithaca. He can, and, as a bonus, you meet
your late mother. You skirt the Sirens' island, stop
your crew's ears with wax, tie yourself to the mast
so none will be seduced by their song. It works.

The body count rises. The six-headed Scylla
seizes a man for each as you pass. You hit
Helios, and despite all your warnings,
the starving crew make a meal of local beef;
so the next storm kills them all, and you're alone.

Fast forward seven years spent with Calypso.
You only escape when other gods intervene,
make her let you go. Poseidon's long memory
sends a storm to wreck your ship, but you
are washed up on Scheria, whose princess
takes you home to Dad. He's impressed,
wants you to wed his daughter. At talk
of Troy, you break down, admit who you are,
accept the offer of a ship to take you home.

Ithaca. You have things to explain to your wife.

ANGELS, 2023

Lacking the strength to shift mountains,
vigour to fight,
the intellect to negotiate,
I sit in quiet comfort making angels.

Each is a part of my vision,
each a herald of peace,
each worked from a pearl face, tiny silver wings,
beads of coloured glass for robe and halo,
a headpin holding it together. All seem
the same, but every one is singular,
different enough to be its own prayer.

One gleams with blue above, yellow below,
hints defiance, freedom from tyranny.
One reflects earth colours, unearthed
as the ground shuddered itself apart.
One bears the unremitting white of plague,
of hospital bed and shroud.
One is the indigo of sea, stained with blood
of foundering, of desperate deaths.
One is robed in purple, crowned in gold,
assuming his mantle in the midst of mourning.

All merge into one prism of grief, one promise of peace,
spread their wings wide to encompass the world.

STAINED GLASS AND SOIL

I contemplate this window,
plain and pitted with age, where sun dazzles;
start by sketching feathery glimpses of tree
across three tall shapes.

                Beyond the glass, unfettered, free,
                an oak is rooted firm in earth.

I structure my design, work a neater image.
Colour comes next, water-based pencils flirting
with the tree's outline, trying fruits,
letting squirrels skitter in its branches.

                Outside each leaf presents
                a different nuance of green.

It's time for the cartoon. Now
my drawing is precise, sized exactly
for each pattern to fit in consecrated stone,
showing where every piece of glass will sit.

                Sun drenches the oak, that reaches
                in joy toward light, to its heat.

I select the lengths of glass,
score with my scalpel, snap them, check
that every piece will add
to the breathtaking whole.

                The trunk shows age, folds and creases
                opening their heart to grub and beetle.

And now, the joy of paint,
learning new depths of colour,
undreamed shades, weights, textures.
My design, no longer concept, finds reality.

> A gentle rain falls,
> adds sheen to every leaf.

It is time to fill the kiln, fire it
over and over until each fragment of glass
glitters ruby and emerald, bright diamond;
glows its own music.

> Blackbirds whistle in highest branches.
> A woodpigeon coos.

The pieces are leaded together,
a thousand years of tradition
forging the jigsaw to be soldered,
fixed in a fusion of tree to glass.

> Snow re-maps the landscape
> with its strange and transient blossom.

Cementing, brushing, cleaning
weatherproofs stained glass panels, makes them solid
to be fitted, to be gasped over, admired
for a hundred years and more.

> Acorns of continuity
> grow, crop, seed.

HAIKU

Midsummer sun spills
molten gold that catches breath;
fills the sea with fire.

THE BOY NEXT DOOR

Early morning. We shuffled soft grass
still damp from dew, our ears
dripping with birdsong, a day of adventure
and daring stretching before us. We left behind
mown lawns and formal rosebeds, turned our gaze
to wilder places that thrilled
our longing to explore.

Rough reed, humps and hillocks,
clumps of dandelion and late wild primrose
spread at our feet. We carried bottles
to fill with tadpoles, nets for catching butterflies,
a box in vain hope of a sand lizard.

And we talked. How we talked. We told tales
of teachers and their evil ways –
compelling homework, good manners, respect,
with their power to administer slaps
and appoint milk monitors. We shared accounts
of the indistinct monochrome of Doctor Who and Blue Peter,
the jokes we'd read in comics.

We were the first Superheroes, spies stalking
deranged villains, Tarzan-swinging
in imagination through jungles
(or those few scrubby trees), millionaires
dressing up as bats. We raced along paths,
hurled ourselves over sand dunes, arrived,
breathless, at the sea
and, heedless of warnings to stay out of the water,
stole an illicit paddle.

We played until hunger drove us home,
up the left drive or the right, demanding lunch
from his Mum or mine. Summer reached
through June, July, kept at bay
September days and back-to-school.

Those years were seamless; endless.
I cannot remember the last sortie, the last chase,
the last time we compared notes
about mean parents who made us do chores,
shortfalls between pocket money
and the treats we wanted to buy.

I cannot remember how things changed,
the day the rough-and-tumble turned
into a kiss, the day his touch
made my fingers fizz.

Years on, grown, aged, married
to other people, we still meet.
We talk. How we talk. We tell tales
of our children, grandchildren, ailments;
a mere breath away
from summer's magic.

OFF THE BRIDGE

I wrapped it in a soft, white scarf,
imagined breaths and heartbeats.
I thought his threats were empty, but
I never saw him again.

Imagined breaths and heartbeats
petrified beneath my fingers,
laced together around that impossible smallness.

I thought his threats were empty, but
his thinking filled a dark, dark place,
a place that offered no alternatives.

I never saw him again,
never went back to that bridge; yet still
the burden weights my bloodless hands.

ALBATROSS

It's time to put the record straight.
Why should a murderer
get so much sympathy? Think.
He's gatecrashed a wedding, bored
an innocent guest into submission,
and all to absolve himself of killing me.

When his vessel stuck in fields of ice
they welcomed me, left me food,
fish and bread, a little meat. I stayed
until ice split, the helmsman could steer
a safe course.

I soared above their ship, rose on thermals,
spread my wings to their full twelve feet.
My presence brought good fortune to those sailors.
The soul I was carrying home fused
with my white-feathered breast,
shimmered blessings over them.

Then the weather turned. There was a haze
in the air – no more. He fixed a bolt. Drew his crossbow.
The pain was agonising, fleeting. I fell to the deck,
became in death their ill omen.

Hanging at his neck, I was blamed when we stalled
on windless sea, when crew members perished
one by one, when his mind disintegrated. Only last and late
his finding prayer let my dead weight drop.

My story lives on in lore of my kind.
New generations know that grudges are futile,
still carry souls back to their maker, still
bring benison to those who ply the sea. Meanwhile
the guilty one's condemned to tell his tale of me
over and over, over and over, while men
who know nothing of oceans and their ways
cannot escape its telling.

THE UNREAD

They stand straight, smug rows
of know-it-all volumes looking down on me
as I browse a newspaper, watch TV or knit.

I was seduced by bright jacketed promises,
spent the money for groceries on books instead,
knew I would be entertained, amused, informed.

How could I have guessed
in the rush of ready-for-school, washing, scrubbing,
meals-on-the-table, tidying, sewing,

those books would gather dust, fox,
fix their air of superiority? Now
as time careers toward my final page,

energy saps, enthusiasm wanes, my mind
crumbles like confetti made of shredded chapters,
but still they lure me, challenge me to touch.

I reach out to those ranks of the undead,
pick out a novel, a how-to, a biography,
resolve to offer them an hour a day.

And then I see not smugness on their spines
but invitation, find how yellowing age
can't compromise the urgent black of print.

I consume. I am consumed,
entertained, amused, informed, fuel-filled,
joy-filled, one with tale and text.

SKY BLUES

Feeling a little dowdy
after days of unremitting grey,
and missing oohs and aahs of appreciation
at dewy sunrise or its gold-tinged setting,
the sky, greedy for compliments,
promised himself a perfect storm.

He conspired with cloud layers
to find a darkening bolder than charcoal,
richer than indigo, to draw attention.
He suggested the sun take a rest to recharge,
and checked moon's angle
for a satisfying sliver.

He demanded that rain
fall only in heaviest drops,
battering windows, ricocheting from roads.
He commanded lightning
to flash giant forks heaven to earth,
setting roofs on fire, terrifying cattle.

He commanded thunder to drum a cadenza,
synchronise with swelling of high tides.

It worked. From every house, every office,
watchers huddled, gasping in awe
as the storm raged, in fear
as thunderclaps crescendoed.

And the sky? He took the wonder,
relished comments, basked in the drama,
and had a quiet word with the sun,
scheduling next day's duck-egg blue.

MEMO

It has been decided
that the dictionary rendering of Woman
as *an adult female human being*
is insufficiently detailed
to serve as an adequate definition.
We are therefore requesting your feedback
on various proposed additions.

Woman: *an adult female human being* ...

who can run a multinational company,
speak seven languages, negotiate contracts,
and knows to the penny
the balance of their joint account.

who can whip up dinner for eight
when she discovers the guests
(her husband forgot to say he'd invited)
are due to arrive in 45 minutes.

who knows the square root of 729,
recites the periodic table by heart,
can name all Peppa Pig's classmates
and informs you that she saw you eat 27 smarties.

can play Chopsticks and Beethoven,
dance a quickstep in 3-inch heels,
put together a pirate fancy dress outfit
with eyepatch, tricorn hat and parrot,
bake a fruitcake without weighing ingredients.

always knows whether tea, tlc or g&t is required,
understands the workings of the universe
and knows when her children
have not done their homework.

Please tick all that apply
and return to Lexicographers Anonymous.

Thank you.

SHIRLEY

I called her Shirley, the nice girl
just a little older than I was, who came
to play, relieve my only-child boredom.

Pretty with golden hair, good at making up stories,
she moved into our home; but I had to remind Mum
to set an extra place for lunch, yell
at Dad not to sit in the armchair on top of her.

Always smiling, always good,
she never had to be told
to ask to leave the table, to brush her teeth,
and she never left the towel
in a soggy heap on the bathroom lino.

My early-formed rebellious streak
would sometimes lose patience,
so I made sure she got the blame
when a jamjar for washing paintbrushes spilt,
when a plate was broken.

I realised she, like me, wrote S back to front
when she scratched my name on the table with a pin.
She could count to twenty, sing songs,
say verses, promised she would come with me
when I started Big School.

And that was when Shirley slipped away.
Big School meant other friends,
new games to play, a house move.

She stayed behind. I had a garden now,
playmates, and suddenly
I was no longer an only child.

Shirley? She still lives in that garden-less
terraced house in town, sings songs
to other children, writes their names on tables.

HAIKU

Dusk shadows lengthen
where drifting sycamore keys
dream Spring's flourishing.

THE GIFT

A pretty gift, he'd chosen it with care,
black flowers and net in flurries of black lace.
I never guessed the secret lurking there.

He lifted up my tumbled auburn hair
and wound the scarf around me, touched my face.
A pretty gift, he'd chosen it with care,

presented with a flourish, and his stare
held all the love I felt in his embrace.
I never guessed the secret. Lurking there

beneath his smile was bitterness, his fair
and honeyed words were cover. As he placed
a pretty gift – he'd chosen it – with care,

I realised he'd learned of my affair.
Black flowers became a symbol of disgrace.
I never guessed the secret lurking there,

how he had sworn revenge. He reached, and where
he grabbed, pulled tight, I fell through blackest space.
A pretty gift. He'd chosen it with care.
I never guessed how death was lurking there.

0.0002%

Of all the water here on earth,
only a fraction falls through streams and rivers,
follows the route from a trickling spring
to jink and swirl around rocks;
and burn, rill, brook, creek, rivulet
have little significance ...

until you realise the Ganges
from time immemorial
has been the sacred river of Hinduism;
Blue Nile, White Nile had to flow
before Egypt could come to life;
more than two thousand miles of Mississippi
meander down to New Orleans
draining over half the states;
the Thames sustained London
through two millennia of history;
Yangtze providing irrigation,
transportation, sanitation
marking boundaries, supporting threatened species.

Stand on any river bank
trying to envisage 0.0002% ...
and imagine a world without it.

THE GRINDYLOW

Where reed-banked rivers run by emerald fields,
or sun dappled, in light
filtered through leaves of oak and beech,
beware the lure of soft teasing ripples
that teem with sticklebacks, froth over stones:
for these bear whispers of the grindylow.

She hides her green skin, camouflaged
when duckweed gathers where the water stills,
and mothers warn their sons and daughters
that Jenny Greenteeth will reach sinewy arms,
wrap spindly fingers tethering their wrists
and drag them under,
hold them below the river's race
until the bubbles of their breathing stop.

Or she will pierce them with her pin-sharp teeth,
snag their skin on riverbed's sharp stones,
bind with her tentacles and bundle them
into some strange demonic cell
where there is no air, no light,
no other sound than water's rush
above their heads.

Appeased by sacrifice, she sinks in slime
at the river's edge, extends her arms as reeds,
wriggles her tentacles to merge with waterweed,
anticipates her next small victim.

INVASION

Beware hordes of gingerbread men
rampaging into your life when first firs
flicker with light. Their intrusion
will be swift, their spice tingling in air,
all on a mission to fill a dark world
with impossibly broad grins.
Teddy-bear-cute, round as a hug,
they slide into fractious moments,
defuse the whose-turn-to-make-tea arguments,
calm the seething, soothe
shopped-out, ruffled nerves. Accept them.
There is nothing you can do. If you corral them,
counter attack by biting their heads off,
you simply unleash back-up troops
of cosy memories, let their warmth
spread through you. Better to give in.
Find a smile to match theirs. Relish,
with them, every remembrance of Christmas Past,
every moment of Christmas Present,
every wish for Christmas Yet to Come.

... BUT ONCE A YEAR

It's always rough this time of year. He moans
and grumbles. I remind him he volunteered
for the job, seduced by the offer of house-on-site
and transport, staff who work for nothing.

That was the year the whole world wanted
Tracy Island – swimming pool and rockets.
We could have done with International Rescue,
I can tell you. Fifty elves were deployed to make
the things, demanding milk and extra candy canes.
He went off on the pre-season recce.
Two billion kids in the world. One billion nice.
Half asked for Tracy Island. We'd made ninety.
So who do you think fields the elves' complaints
of being overworked? Who's supplying
chocolate with marshmallows
twenty-four/seven? Me of course.

I'd said when he took the job
the sleigh had seen better days. Rusty bodywork,
suspension shot, exhaust knackered –
and when you're powered by nine reindeer,
there's a lot of waste gas to be vented. He'd hardly
got to Moscow when the brakes failed.

'You'll have to take a bunch of those elves to help'
I'd told him, but would he listen?
'I've got the magic' he kept saying.
He'd also got the indigestion.
Two billion mince pies
mean a heap of pastry for one colon.

He limped in around mid-day. A bit merry.
Who am I fooling? Plastered. He swallowed
a whole pack of Rennies and slept the clock round.

It's more or less the same every year.
New crazes, same grumbles.
And would either of us swap it?
Never.

A CANDLE FOR ADVENT

We burn a little every day,
watch as wax pools, drips through the numbers
two, three, five,
each snuffing a reminder of time squeezing
the hours out of my days, each number
reflecting warnings on last-day-to-mail leaflets.

I sense the shopping list edging
into panic mode, know delays
six, eight,
will only presage last minute decisions
without a glance at prices.

The shortened candle compresses
nine, ten. eleven,
and fears of no eggs for baking,
no potatoes for roasting,
no turkeys for basting,
no bottles for forgetting
fill my shrinking thoughts.

I start to dream of lists that will not be completed,
of not-wrapped presents, unanswered calls,
standing naked in the kitchen
thirteen, fifteen,
wondering where it all went wrong.

My thoughts unravel
to puddle in chaos at my feet
nineteen, twenty, twenty-two,
and I wonder what would happen
if I made the call,
made an excuse to the world,
tried to fall off.

Twenty four.
I'm still here. It will happen.
I have neither fallen nor been pushed.
I'll save the panic for New Year.

JANUARY

This is not the time
for sloe-eyed lingering on Christmas-just-past,
laments of baubles packed in bubble wrap
in case you are still here next year.

Today slaps snow to sting warm cheeks,
shouts that cards need ripping up,
that unbuttered bread and plain soup
wait to celebrate the turkey's end.

Fling open the curtains of your mind,
expel to-do lists that were never done.
Fight too-early dusk with brisk walks,
not lamplight and a last mince pie.

Shake the bells and carols from your ears
and fill them with the raucous calls
of early-nesting magpies, murmur
of roots trying hard earth.

January sprawls its promise,
a spread of year to colour in
with patchworked moments, sighs, songs,
tantrums, laughter, and a weave of love.

TEN WAYS OF LOOKING AT A SLUG
(with apologies to Wallace Stevens)

Black and silken,
you ooze through wet grass.

You fear nothing
except salt.

Alone, you can produce
a hundred eggs a year.

If you don't move, if you don't breathe,
the hedgehog will shuffle past.

A gastropod, you belong
to the second largest family on earth.

You can strip my delphiniums,
turn their leaves to lace.

You eat forty times your body's weight
in a day.

Invisible until twilight, you lurk
in plain sight, melt in the eye's periphery.

Coming from water, comprising water,
you can only move through your trail's slime.

Your swan song squelches
beneath an unforgiving foot.

A QUESTION OF EVE

I have always wondered about Eve;
formed from the rib of (male) Adam as his plaything,
given no rights over the naming of creatures or flowers,
left to negotiate with a (male) serpent,
and face the wrath of a (male) deity,
how outnumbered must she have felt?

And after the whistleblower
ratted her out to God, she was blamed
for eviction from the garden. No matter
how many figleaves she wove together,
she was the one who got pregnant,
with no other woman
to tell her why she bled; to tell her why she didn't.

She, who had never been a child,
who had never known a child,
must have suckled by instinct,
held her son close to stop his crying,
taught him obedience, in fear
of consequences she knew too well.

How did she process pain,
when one (male) child she loved
killed the other (male) child she loved?
How did she know how to love?
How did she know how to mourn?

I always wondered about Eve,
but with nobody able to answer the questions,
drew my own conclusions. She (female) worked.
She (female) learned. She (female) knew.

REBOOT

I have decided to reboot my life,
to check through all the error messages,
address them, eliminate them.

A simple switch it off, switch it on again
is not enough. I shall return myself
to manufacturer's settings.

When I am tempted to eat too much,
drink too much, return to an overweight status quo,
I shall find my Control F shortcut
and choose a stick of celery instead.

When I feel depressed and miserable
I shall Google 'Things to Make me Happy',
and take delight from the fact
that point-six-of-a-second
yields four million responses.

When I feel lazy,
can't be bothered to make toast for breakfast,
go to work, feed the cat,
I shall press alt and tab,
take myself back to the last scenario.

And when I know
that the reboot has been successful,
that I am a new and lovely person,
not greedy, not sad and not idle,
I'll freeze my screen
and save my settings,
fully charged.

A WORD OF APOLOGY ...

Dear Granny

This is just a little note
Mum thought I should write
to say I'm sorry. When I met that wolf
and told him where I was going,
I had no idea he'd run ahead and scare you.

I'm sorry he broke into your cottage
and pushed you into the wardrobe. Sorry
he climbed into your bed
and left muddy pawmarks on the sheets.
Mum says your nightdress
still smells of wolf,
even though you've washed it twice.

I'm sorry about the mess
when the woodsman came in with his axe.
Wolves must have a lot of blood.
I hope you managed to scrub the carpet clean.

I'm sorry that, in all the excitement,
I dropped the basket of cakes and pies
Mum sent for you.

I promise that next time I meet a wolf I won't tell him
you live alone in your cottage in the wood.
I'll suggest he goes along the other path
where those little pigs have built their houses.

Lots of love from
Red   xx

STYX

In seven circlings of the underworld
she formed a border, ever to divide
the living from the dead. Her waters swirled
and stormed, while Charon crossed from side to side
to ferry all the bodies who could pay
the coin that he demanded. For the rest,
they wandered on her banks a year, a day
as wraiths in limbo, unloved and unblessed.
To fall in her meant hatred, dreams dispelled.
To bathe in her gave strength and speed and might.
An oath gods swore on her must be upheld
on threat of exile from Olympus' height.
    She's flowed through space and time – her destiny
    to keep the dead contained, the living free.

HAIKU

Storm rages; passes.
One flattened early crocus
struggles upright. Spring.

LEAP YEAR DAY

It's a gift
from Julius Caesar,
a day out of time
to freewheel in, wallow in,
wonder at, wish about,
work through or waste.

It's a present for everyone,
twenty-four hours
that have silently gathered
as earth's spin made fractions
confusing, bemusing
our skewed calculations.

It's a chance to propose
or to dance, or to dine
while winter's last gasps
wheeze the end of their days
as they wait
for the warming of spring.

So diary it, celebrate,
cogitate, swim in it,
swallow it, hallow it,
fill it with fun and frivolity,
jollity, laughter and games.
It's a gift.

ANOTHER PLACE

Seasoned travellers, these hundred
six-foot-two-inch Gormley clones,
cast iron images of his naked body
each weighing the same as ten men, stand sentinel.
They have gazed out from Cuxhaven,
Stavanger, De Panne, and now near Liverpool
they stare across the Mersey, all looking out
into an untried future, into another place.

Spreading along two miles of foreshore,
deep into the sea, they are prey
to vagaries of tides,
sometimes beached, sometimes awash,
trying to stand, trying to breathe
in swirls of water.

Lines of ships pass in and out,
weighed down with cargo, weighted
with the woes and joys
of tired commuters, eager visitors.
The iron army almost winks.

Passing seasons colour the sky
slate grey to duck-egg blue, balance
sun brightness with pinpoint stars,
and still they gaze, ankle deep, thigh deep.

Part of the community,
they are hailed by those who walk the shore,
crowned by screeching gulls,
dressed in red scarves, blue scarves
for football, white coats for cricket.

Weathered by sea's pounding
they bear scars in weed and rust,
are colonised by sea creatures in the brine,
by dogs on the sand, children
bearing buckets and spades,
trippers and snappers.

Still they wait, still they age
exposing their vulnerability,
believing in survival
but pondering the meaning of life.

They show us more about ourselves
than we could ever guess.

THE LAST LAUGH

He was the clever one, my brother,
pocketing chips of flint to drop a trail
when Father's wicked wife plotted
to abandon us, lost in the forest. Moonlight
silvered the chippings, lit our way home.

He was the clever one, my brother,
laying a trail of breadcrumbs when she tried
her evil trick again. But how could Hansel know
that birds would steal our markers? Lost and wandering,
we stumbled on, followed where a bright bird flew.

He was the clever one, my brother,
discovering a cottage made of gingerbread,
tearing chunks from the roof before we starved.
And when the crone caught us, lured us in, locked him
in a cage, forced me to fatten him up,
he thought to cheat her failing sight
swapping fleshless bone for his fleshly finger.

He was the clever one, my brother,
for after I'd tricked the witch into her own oven
and fastened it shut, he, freed,
ransacked her gingerbread house for the gold and pearls,
rubies and emeralds, rewards for her crimes,
loaded them into my pockets and apron.

He was the clever one, but he dismissed
his sweet little sister, who led him safe back to the river,
persuaded a snow white duck to ferry us over,
found the way home where we learned of the curse
that had baited and killed our stepmother. I say nothing
of that. I smile at my father, smile at my brother,
smile at the thought of that fine stash of jewels. Smile.

AND I DO FEAR ...

I told him not to go to work today.
I begged him, for the omens were so dire.
Of course he wouldn't simply make excuse,
too principled to lie, too sensible
to listen to the ravings of his wife.
If he'd believed me, if he'd stayed at home,

tonight he would be dining, drinking wine,
or strolling in the moonlight. But instead
he's lying lifeless on a stone, with blood
in rust-dry spatters on his cloak, his toga.
I wasn't asking much; a single lie.
Mark Antony was set to take his place,
and all he did was tell me that the brave
will never taste of death but once. But once
is once too many. Oh, my dear, dead lord,
I saw this happen in a nightmare, cried
three times that you were stabbed. You still ignored.
I told you of the lioness who birthed
her cubs out in the street, of graves that gaped
and spewed their rotting contents into air,
and nothing that I said could make you stay.

So he is gone and I must bear the curse
of wondering if anything I said,
some new plea, more insistence, could have saved
him from this fate. I did my best: forgave
his dalliance with that Egyptian whore,
his absences for fighting, leading men
to war away from home and family.

I told him not to go to work today.
Tomorrow brings the worst of work for me;
the task of burying my husband, mourned
by many, stabbed by those he thought were friends.
I'll wear my veil, stand firm, and never weep,
but inwardly I'll curse the Ides of March.

THREE DAYS

I still can't believe he did it -
running off like that without a word. We'd been every year,
every year since he was a toddler newly back from Egypt.
It was like a big family party, all of us
trekking to Jerusalem for the Passover Festival
and all on a joyous journey home, walking
with this one and that, chatting, relishing the company.

I blame myself for the day it took
to realise he wasn't with us, not with our relatives,
nor any neighbours. I can still taste
panic rising like vomit in my throat, still shiver
with chills of terror despite relentless sun.

We half stumbled, half ran back to the city,
Joseph saying little, but I knew
he was as worried as I, he too felt he was to blame.
Then came the searching; the place we'd stayed,
the inns, bazaar, anywhere a boy might play.
Three days. Three whole days we looked for him.
Perhaps we were wrong to leave the temple to last,
a sort of desperation, knowing if we had no hope of finding him
there would be solace in prayer within its courts.

And there he was. Contrite? No.
Full of apologies? No. Just that look
only a twelve-year-old can deliver,
and that smug 'Didn't you know
I'd be in my Father's house?'

So what do you do? I wanted to hug him.
I wanted to slap him. No-one wrote the book
of how to raise the son of God.

We turned again towards Nazareth.
The journey gave us all space for reflection.
He must have noticed how upset I'd been.
He was good, respectful when we got home.
And of course, the love I had for him deepened.
But I'd learned: three days can be a very long time.

THE LAST CASE

One of earth's saddest sights
is the last suitcase on the airport carousel
trundling its route past tired travellers.

Think of it: lovingly packed in Rome
or Geneva or Las Vegas, cossetting
the bubble-wrapped saint, or watch,
or the last chip, wrapped in a week's washing.

It bears with pride the scars
inflicted by gung-ho baggage handlers,
or clumsy cleaners with sharp-cornered vacuums.
It is locked, and wrapped in garish straps
so nobody will mistake it for theirs.

A short length of string, still attached,
shows where an address label was.

The carousel sighs
as it starts another circuit,
dizzies the case with a consolatory spin,
conspires with its desolation. It has seen
all this before.

Arrivals empties. Distracted parents, yawning children
are trudging toward their final destination.
Only a customs official stands there,
stretches, sees the case
start yet another round.

Tomorrow, somebody will notice
there's something missing. Somebody
will call the airport, claim their case.

Tonight, hopes fading,
it lies neglected, rejected,
wheels and handles retracted,
a metaphor for regret.

BREATHING THE SEA

She runs down the beach
three and free, loosed from her pushchair,
loosed from my hand, launches herself
towards sea so vast
its next land is Africa.

I call. She ignores. I yell.
She runs faster, hurls herself
into the breaking waves.
Now I heave my skirt high around my waist,
hurtle after her, legs too old for running
finding a speed they've never known,
bare feet tripping me up.

Shock of water slows her,
lets me catch her up,
hug her in my arms, my head and heart
full of memories of a dive-gone-wrong,
my lungs bursting again,
my desperate race to beat the depth,
beat the dark, reach healing sun.

She squirms, wiggles wet toes,
laughs the sheer exuberance of water
and I set her down, her feet
sinking with mine
through tide-ripped sand.

The afternoon buckets and spades
into laughter and paddles,
bottled water sipped, shells gathered,
stones arranged to form her H. I look
beyond the distant waves, feel Africa
on my cheek, let choking fears dissolve,
know again a mother's terror
for the fragility of breath and bones.

MOVING DAY

This is the final moment. I'm here alone,
checking lights are off, windows are shut
through this house where I never lived
but always called home.

Now everything is done, and I sit five stairs up,
sink my head to my knees. I can hear my Dad
whistling in his workshop, as he finds promises
of gifts to craft in the grain of wood. I can smell
roasting beef as Mum prepares
Sunday lunch for ten, anticipate
the hotcold thrill of Baked Alaska
I will never taste again.

I can see myself relaxing on the sofa with my sister,
chatting over a glass of wine, laughing,
content and confident in the love
that permeates this place.

I remember all the joy of family parties,
Christmas dinners, birthday teas, Pimms in the garden,
games and stories, occasional tears
dried before they fell. I remember the day
we sat at the table and told them
of the new grandchild to come, the day we dressed my sister
for her wedding, and when we strolled to the gate to wave
as the Queen of England was driven past.

I remembered how we gathered here in silence,
climbed into black limousines to see our Father, Mother
leaving this house for the last time.

No, I never lived here, but my heart did.
And as I leave the key, go out, slam the door,
I know I'm leaving the best of me behind.

Printed and bound by CPI Group (UK) Ltd, Croydon, CR0 4YY
01/11/2024
01782780-0004